ICE AGE ™

The Essential Guide

SCRAT

MANNY

SID

DIEGO

EDDIE

CRASH

ICE AGE™

The Essential Guide

Written by Glenn Dakin

Contents

Welcome to the Ice Age!

Pack some warm clothes and watch your step, because you are now entering the Ice Age. The weather forecast predicts snow (for the next few million years) with occasional large-scale floods. But don't despair, it's not all bad news. If you stick around (and don't get eaten or go extinct) you could make some really cool friends.

So enjoy your trip – you'll find the Ice Age a great place to chill out.

Manny

Pouffy hair

Manfred the woolly mammoth is the most faithful and loyal friend anyone could ask for. He is also moody, grouchy and stubbornly determined to go it alone.

Sharp tusks

Manny's trunk is more like an extra finger!

Short, furry tail

Woolly feet

Mammoth issues

Manny has a few "issues": He stubbornly refuses to believe that mammoths are going extinct. He also hates to be called fat – he says it's just his fur that makes him look "kind of pouffy".

8

These cave paintings remind Manny of his sad secret. They also help Sid and Diego to understand why he is such a hard guy to get to know.

Family secret

Manny's mate and child were killed by hunters. Since then he has been alone, but when he meets Ellie, Manny starts to wonder if he could be happy again. First he must convince her that she is a mammoth, not a possum!

Manny is great at being grumpy, but gets trunk-tied when it comes to love. Luckily, he and Ellie are well-suited – they're both stubborn and come with annoying baggage!

"I'm not going extinct!"

Ice Age hero

Manny is a good guy. He protects Roshan from sabre-toothed tigers and leaps into a whirlpool to save Ellie. Perhaps his bravest act of all is putting up with Sid!

A Mammoth Attitude

Manny is the Ice Age's biggest grouch. He hates animals like Soto, who kill for pleasure; bullies, like the rhinos, who pick on weaker animals; sneaky conmen, like Fast Tony and doom-mongers, like the vultures. He even dislikes his own pals most of the time!

Manny has found a pal for life, whether he likes it or not! Tactful as always, Sid advises Manfred to reinvent himself as "Manny the Moody Mammoth".

"You are my problem!"

Tusks are great for sweeping aside snow to reach food.

Manny and man

Manny has little time for humans. He hates their "modern architecture" and he's sure it will never last. He just can't understand how humans survive when they have no fangs and are just made of skin and "mush".

When Manny met Ellie

When they first meet, Manny thinks Ellie is stubborn, infuriating and narrow-minded – in other words, he's crazy about her! Ellie notices that they have a lot in common and wonders if Manny is part possum! Well, no one ever said that love was easy...

Pesky pal

Sid really doesn't mind when Manny says he's just a pesky, conniving freeloader. Sid has learnt to take deeply offensive personal remarks as a sign of interest in him.

Sloths have sharp claws. Sid finds them handy for scratching fleas!

Sid

Fire god, cave artist, hilarious joker, ladies' man – that's how Sid likes to think of himself. But Sid is a sloth. He is lazy, greedy, smelly and insensitive, and those are his better qualities! He is a magnet for trouble, fun and fur fungus.

Beady eyes are always on the lookout for a free lunch!

Lord of the flame

For once, Sid did something useful and discovered how to make fire. However, Manny and Diego's surprise soon turned to laughter as Sid set his own tail on fire. Little did those guys know that Sid would turn out to be a genuine fire god!

The smell of barbecued sloth is likely to attract predators.

Shaggy fur needs serious grooming

When Sid drew a self-portrait, Manny said it would be more realistic if the figure was lying down.

Sid is a surprisingly good babysitter. Childish pranks, dribble and stinky smells can be a problem, but baby Roshan soon learns to put up with them.

SLOTH FACTS

• The average tree sloth spends 75% of its time sleeping and eating, but Sid can easily beat this record.

• Most sloths freeze absolutely still when in danger, but Sid can't even stay quiet for five minutes!

Ladies' sloth

Sid will try any sneaky tactic to impress female sloths. He even uses a cute human baby to melt the hearts of the ladies at the hot springs. Sid just can't understand why a cool guy like him can't find a mate!

Being impaled by an icicle is just a joke to Sid, but Soto isn't going to find it funny later on...

"I'm a genius!"

Ice Age dandelion

Sid has an eye for trouble!

Sharp teeth for shredding leaves

Here comes trouble

Sid can't seem to stay out of trouble. When he spots a delicious dandelion, he thinks it's his lucky day and gobbles it right up. Two hungry rhinos can't quite believe their eyes...

Sloth Survival Guide

When you're the slowest-moving creature on the planet, with no fangs, armoured plates or poisonous spines for protection, you have to be pretty clever to survive. Or in Sid's case, you just have to get by on good old-fashioned luck!

In dangerous situations, Sid can produce an amazing speed-waddle, which can sometimes cause predators to die laughing.

Making enemies

Sid is such a natural at annoying everybody that even vegetarians are out to get him. Two rhinos, Frank and Carl, were not pleased when Sid ruined their salad. Thankfully, Sid has backup – Manny.

"We'll have some fun with him."

Frank has one big horn.

Carl's horn has scary double point.

"I'm putting sloths on the map!"

Joke ice-fangs offer no survival advantages and can cause gum sores.

To escape angry sabre-toothed tigers Sid invents skis, thousands of years ahead of humans.

Survival tips
Carnivores love fresh meat, so Sid's trick is to smell so bad that most predators take one sniff and think he's been rotting for weeks.

If in doubt, make your natural enemies feel you are too stupid to be worth eating. Attempting to create a fire in a rainstorm works for Sid.

The Sabre Gang

They may be furry, but these sabre-toothed tigers certainly aren't cuddly. Meet the guys Diego used to hang out with before he found a new pack. Led by the seriously scary Soto, these fang-faced friends love eating out – as long as the food doesn't fight back too hard!

No that's not a sabre-sized toothpick, it's a human spear – something even Soto and his gang have learnt to fear.

The boss

Soto hates humans because they kill sabre-toothed tigers and wear their furs to keep warm. He is determined to take revenge on humans.

Big cat

Lumbering Lenny loves his food. He's actually a rare scimitar cat, so don't call him a sabre-toothed tiger – it might make him mad.

Zeke is the smallest cat in the pack.

Wild and crazy, Zeke is a simple cat who likes nothing more than a good mauling.

Cat fight

As one of Soto's best hunters, Diego was happy to follow the pack. But when Diego chooses to help a baby, a mammoth and a sloth instead of his pack, Soto is very angry. He tries to make Diego pay with his life.

"I'll take you down first."

Clever plan

When Manny and Sid find the baby before Diego, he comes up with a mean idea. He plans to steal the baby and also deliver his pack a tasty treat – Manny!

Diego

Diego was Soto's most trusted tracker. But when it comes to bringing home a human baby for his cruel pack leader, Diego shows his true nature. He realizes that loyalty and friendship are more important than revenge.

"GGRRRRRR"

Extra-long sabre tooth

A real pussycat

This snarling tough guy has a good heart. He respects Manny's feelings when Sid keeps raising the subject of family or talking about extinction. Diego also secretly loves playing peek-a-boo with baby Roshan.

SABRE FACTS

- The sabre is not closely related to tigers at all – it's really a type of cat!
- Sabres could be up to 3 m (10 ft) long and weigh as much as 200 kg (450 lb).
- Sabres' fangs grew up to 25 cm (10 in) long and jaws opened extra wide for awesome biting power.

Scaredy-cat

Not much scares Diego, except being plunged into freezing water. Sabres just don't "do" water, OK? It takes an unusual swimming lesson from Sid to convince him that swimming is really just like stalking any other prey.

Short, powerful legs, perfect for stalking prey

Tempting moment

Diego's new-found nice-guy image is put to the test when he puts Sid in his mouth to fool two angry rhinos. As Sid plays dead, Diego can't help feeling hungry. Fortunately, Manny shows up before Diego can fall back into his old ways.

Huge, sharp claws

Baby Talk

He may look like a small, helpless baby, but this cool kid has picked up some survival skills. How many other humans have survived playing peek-a-boo with a sabre-toothed tiger, taken a ride on a woolly mammoth and been babysat by a sloth?

- Ice Age humans were very skilled – they could hunt, make tools and create fire.
- There were no sweets or cake in the Ice Age, but the clever humans used honey to make their food taste sweeter.

Soft human skin

Home is a hut made of wood and animal skins.

"Pinky"

Known to Manny, Sid and Diego as "Pinky", the baby's real name is Roshan. He is the son of Runar and Nadia and his survival is vital to the future of his tribe.

Clothes made from animal skin

Humans

Life in the Ice Age wasn't easy for humans. Conditions were harsh and dangerous. Roshan's tribe is always on the move, hunting bison, mammoths, sabre-toothed tigers and big-horn elk to feed and clothe them.

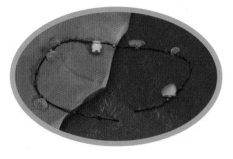

Runar finds Roshan's necklace and keeps it safe, hoping that his son will return home.

Nadia loves her son more than anything. She bravely leaps into the waterfall to prevent the sabre-toothed tigers from harming her baby. Unfortunately, she cannot save herself.

"You're a brave little squirt!"

The rescue

Nadia hopes that Manny and Sid will take care of her son. Sid immediately falls in love with the cute baby, but Manny takes some more convincing.

The First Journey

Sid thinks the whole "Going South" idea is overrated – he just can't stand the heat and the crowds! But it would have been easier than the road north. To get baby Roshan home, Sid and his best buddies encounter ice, fire and some pretty strange folk.

The Road South – bring all your family but leave your "issues" behind.

Sid's tree – his family left him behind on migration day!

This is where Manny and Sid rescue Roshan.

Glacier caves

Sid is chilly but this dinosaur is frozen solid! In the caves, Manny, Sid and Diego find some things that didn't make it to the Ice Age.

Wild Ride

They didn't have roller coasters in the Ice Age but these icy tunnels are the next best thing. Thanks to baby Roshan Manny, Sid and Diego take the ride of their lives through tunnels worn into the glaciers by ancient rivers. The landing is not soft for everyone, but it's definitely worth getting a frozen butt!

Unlimited fun!

There are no height requirements in this Ice Age fun park and the only thing to stop Roshan from riding it all day is Manny – if he can catch up with him!

This is to certify that

DIEGO

has ridden the **Wild Ride.**

Fear turns into joy for Diego as the fur-raising ride brings out the big cub in him! Sadly, Manny and Sid don't share his desire to do it all again.

Team sport

Manny, Sid and Diego may have invented a whole new sport, as they show just how fast a mixed-animal toboggan team can go! However, Manny is not too keen on any future rides – those sabre-toothed tiger and sloth claws are far too rough on his sensitive mammoth hide.

"Whoooooooa! Yeah! Woo!"

Volcano Pass

Is that rumbling noise Sid's stomach? No, unfortunately it is the sound of molten lava erupting far below the ice field. Within seconds, the glacier melts away, leaving only a narrow ice bridge over the boiling-hot lava. Manny, Sid and Roshan safely reach the other side, but Diego is not so lucky.

The Ice Age is a very weird era. One minute everything is icy cold, the next Sid's foot feels a little warm and it's lava time. Sid should have realized that thunder doesn't usually come from underground...

A helping trunk

Just as Diego is about to slip over the edge, Manny comes back and risks his own life to save him. At this moment, Diego realizes he has found a true friend. The sabre-toothed tigers will just have to find another free lunch!

"That's what you do in a herd."

A Strange Herd

There are some weird creatures roaming the Ice Age, but none quite so strange as this trio of mammoth, sloth and sabre-toothed tiger. Manny is the father-figure, wise and strong. Sid provides entertainment and has a knack for landing everyone in trouble. Diego is a great tracker whose teeth and claws are handy in a fight. Life is certainly never dull in this herd!

Manny sometimes regrets being a hero – after all, it did land him with Sid!

It takes something pretty scary to freak out these guys but in the Ice Age, something pretty scary happens every five minutes!

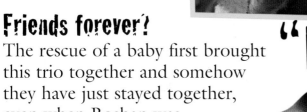

Friends forever?

The rescue of a baby first brought this trio together and somehow they have just stayed together, even when Roshan was returned safely to his father.

"Aaaarrrrggghhhh!"

Furry trunk doubles as a baby sling

Diego is always ready to leap into action.

Sid is never far from panic.

Sabre-cat claws can even grip mammoth hide.

Mammoths have a funny domed head, which they try to hide behind a cool hairdo.

Sloth claws are designed to hang onto almost anything.

Herds rule!

Animals form herds because it makes hunting for food easier. But the best thing is that you get to spend all your time with your best buddies. As for Sid, he loves having two tough guys to watch his back – and boy, does it need watching!

Ice Age Folk

Manny, Sid and Diego meet some strange and wonderful creatures during their journey with Roshan. Some think that the trip south to warmer regions is just a big holiday. While others, like the dodos, are so busy making plans for the future that they forget to watch where they're going today...

Useless wings – dodos can't fly!

The dodos believe that the icy temperatures will force them to live underground for a million-billion years, so they have gathered a stockpile of food – 3 melons.

Huge beak for screeching in panic

Crackpots

The dodos have formed a highly trained army to prepare for the Ice Age. Sadly, it just means they stay perfectly in step as they march off cliffs.

"Doom on you!"

Tae-Kwon dodo!

The dodos are ready for action! These crazy birds will go to any lengths to protect their precious supply of melons – except remember to stay alive.

Big feet

"Give me a break."

Hard outer shell

Large feet

ICE AGE FACTS

• It's thanks to fossils preserved in tar pits that we have such amazing records of the creatures who roamed the Ice Age.

• Dodos had wings but did not know how to fly!

• Glyptodons are relatives of modern-day armadillos.

Slow coaches

The glyptodons are as big as a modern-day car but much less speedy. Despite their hard shells, their feelings are easily hurt.

"We've been waddling all day."

These start kids aren't drowning in the tar pit, they're playing their favourite game – "Extinction".

Extra-long ears

Trunk envy

Manny has the longest trunk around, so he isn't impressed when the short-snouts snipe at him. "If my trunk was that small," he says, "I wouldn't draw attention to myself!"

Short trunk

The Meltdown

When Manny and Diego help out at Campo del Sid, the three buddies little suspect that their whole world is about to become one big waterpark! Their soggy slog to safety never gets dull, with marauding marine reptiles on their tails and some interesting new pals to meet along the way.

This rickety rock-pile is where Manny and Ellie finally touch trunks.

The Geyser Grounds – one false move and you'll be a steamed dinner!

The boat – please form an orderly stampede for boarding.

This crack and the Scrat can change the course of the Ice Age!

A New Age

As the snow begins to melt, the Ice Age world is changing fast and once again it is a place of grass and flowers. The animals that have made it through the long winter have to face a whole new set of challenges. Instead of snowball fights and frostbite, they have to cope with puddle-jumping, hay fever and avoiding defrosted reptiles.

Unfortunately, a wetter world isn't everyone's idea of fun. Diego thinks he can hide his fear of water – not with Sid around!

A refreshing change

This world suits a laid-back guy like Manny. He can graze in the meadows or blend in among the trees if he wants to hide from the crowds (and Sid!) However, Manny will discover that the new world is just as much hassle as the old one!

"The ice is melting!"

Less pouffy hair than Manny's

Ellie

Furry, friendly and, let's face it, a little flaky, Ellie has a small problem – she thinks she's a possum! Her "brothers", Crash and Eddie, have taught her some useful survival tips, like playing dead and how to sleep hanging from a tree, but her main fear is that she will be carried off by a hungry bird!

"I'm a possum!"

Ellie does everything her possum brothers do, but they draw the line at giving her piggy-back rides – especially after what happened to Grandma...

Long, woolly trunk

Large mammoth feet

Large butt

EVEN MORE MAMMOTH FACTS

- A female mammoth was called a cow.
- A female mammoth carried a baby for 22 months before giving birth.
- Female mammoths had smaller tusks than males.

True love?

Ellie and Manny get off to a bad start. Ellie thinks mammoths are stupid for being brave and she gets angry when Manny puts her brother, Crash, in danger. When Manny tries to charm her by telling her that she has a big butt, it looks like this woolly pair will never be anything but enemies...

Eddie

Attacking a sabre-toothed tiger with a pea-shooter is nothing to this feisty furball. Slightly less crazy than his brother, Eddie will still do pretty much anything, as long as there's a promise of a nice roll in the dung patch afterwards.

"Banzai!"

Tail is perfect for swinging from branches

Possum power

Running away or playing dead comes naturally to possums because they will use any sneaky trick to survive. Bravery is considered to be a very foolish thing in the possum community.

Long, hand-like claws for branch gripping

Eddie has a distinctive stripe and a pointed nose.

Don't tell anyone, but Eddie has been known to guzzle too much meltwater before he goes to sleep, which has resulted in occasional tree-wetting problems...

Crash

This disaster-prone daredevil will try any crazy stunt as long as his brother Eddie is there to scrape him off the floor afterwards. He loves his big sister Ellie and will do anything to protect her – even pick fights with guys ten times his size!

Big eyes for night vision

Big nose for smelling danger

Crash knows they can get away with just about anything while their big sister, Ellie, is around.

POSSUM FACTS

• Possums are marsupials, which means that mothers carry their babies in little pouches, just like kangaroos.

• Possums are still around today, but during the Ice Age, they were often eaten by humans.

Crash has a rounded nose and no stripe.

Pale stripes for camouflage

Thumblike hind toe aids gripping

Playing possum

Crash's finest hour so far is convincing Manny to catapult him out of a tree and almost ending up as possum purée! He also invents Ice Age golf and causes an avalanche.

Maelstrom

This freaky reptile defrosted during the big meltdown. He has had millions of years between meals and is ready to make up for lost time! His colossal appetite is matched only by the space between his ears, as his brain is the size of a pea. Still, as Stu the glyptodon soon discovers, it's no longer a good idea to go paddling...

NO SWIMMING

Ice Age creatures don't need any warning signs to tell them when Maelstrom's around – they can smell his fishy breath.

Bony spikes, for protection

Flippers – for propulsion and handing out a slap

Sharp spikes

Mean eyes

*Long jaw, like
a crocodile*

Cretaceous

Named after the era when marine
reptiles ruled the seas, Cretaceous
is not the kind of creature you want
to meet when out for a nice swim. It's
hard to believe that this scary guy ends
up as sushi for the mini-sloths.

REPTILE FACTS

• Cretaceous is a pliosaur
– one of the most savage
predators ever.

• Maelstrom is an
ichthyosaur – a fish-eating
reptile with submarine-like
armour!

• Turtles and sea snakes
are the only sea reptiles
alive today.

"Good sushi!"

Worth waiting for

These ravenous reptiles can't
believe their luck when they
thaw out in an era full of
soft, tasty little mammals.
Unfortunately, nature has
moved on a little since
these two were last awake,
and dining out isn't quite
as easy as they hoped!

DANGER

REPTILES AHEAD

The Food Chain

When the snow falls and food is hard to find, there's one important thing to remember – just where you fit in the food chain! In hard times, your friendly neighbour may decide to invite you to dinner. But be sure to check the menu carefully or you might find your own name on it!

View from the top

Manny and Ellie are sitting pretty on top of the food chain, with only hungry humans to watch out for.

SABRE-TOOTHED TIGERS

To these big guys, the Ice Age is just a big steakhouse, and they can't wait to order a juicy mammoth T-bone!

POSSUMS

The food chain wouldn't be the same without crazy characters like these. You'd have to be pretty hungry to catch them!

MAMMOTHS

Mammoths are kind-hearted vegetarians, with no plans to eat any passers-by. That's why they make such great pals.

SLOTHS

Sleepy sloths are sitting targets for predators. Sid relies on his body odour and irritating personality to put off diners.

HUMANS

The real top of the Ice Age food chain, humans will eat almost anything. Their favourite method of cooking is barbecuing.

DODOS

Plump, tasty and slow, these birdbrains might as well have been born with cooking instructions printed on them!

SCRATS

Since this skinny squirrel never gets to eat any acorns, he doesn't make much of a snack. Anyway, this one bites back!

Scrat

Whatever you do, don't come between a scrat and his nut! This creature will stop at nothing to get his claws on an acorn, whether glaciers, dams or volcanoes stand in his way. With this natural talent for disaster, it's no wonder you don't see any scrats today.

The scrat can't speak, so he tries to communicate through mime. Unfortunately, Sid and Roshan are terrible at guessing games!

The scrat could survive for centuries buried in ice – though the nut would be past its nibble-by date.

The scrat is suffering from a little water retention. Survival tip: If you are planning to bury your acorn, never, ever bury it in a melting glacier wall!

An unlikely hero
When Manny and his pals are in serious danger from a terrible flood, the feisty little scrat proves to be an unexpected (and accidental!) saviour.

Spindly claws ideal for clutching acorns

"EEEEKK!"

SCRAT FACTS

- A scrat is an imaginary sabre-toothed squirrel.
- Squirrels really did exist in the Ice Age and were hunted by man.
- Squirrels eat 800 acorns per year, although the scrat would have been content with just one!

Super-sensitive nut-seeking nose

Super scrat

A scrat never quits! When stomped on by immense creatures like glyptodons, the scrat has the amazing ability to survive without a scratch.

The inedible wood part protects the delicious nut.

The acorn

Acorns are high in fat, carbohydrates and calcium. When they sense winter coming, scrats have a great urge to bury acorns to eat later. Just imagine how crazy this urge gets when a whole Ice Age is coming...

A New Herd

When Manny and Ellie finally get together, Sid and Diego think it's the end of the road for their herd. In fact, it's just the beginning of an even wackier posse! With the addition of Ellie and her two possum brothers, the gang turns into a fully-fledged, happily dysfunctional Ice Age family.

Survival of the fattest

Before this stubborn pair get together, they have to resolve their mammoth issues. Manny has to say goodbye to his old family while Ellie has to accept that she's not a possum. Most importantly, they have to be together because they want to, not just as a convenient way of avoiding extinction!

It looks like Ellie and Manny are Mum and Dad of the new herd. Sid is just a big kid anyway and asks he can have a dog. Manny says no – don't they already have a big cat to worry about?

Woodland camouflage stripes are not much use on a glacier!

If this gang ever stops arguing among themselves, they'll find some challenges ahead – surfing the great flood, escaping the savage jaws of Cretaceous and not ending up as a family meal for a hungry old vulture!

Locked trunks are a traditional mammoth sign of affection.

Powerful front legs great for steering floes

Splayed claws ideal for ice-surfing

LONDON, NEW YORK, MUNICH,
MELBOURNE AND DELHI

Senior Designer Dan Bunyan
Project Editor Catherine Saunders
Publishing Manager Simon Beecroft
Brand Manager Lisa Lanzarini
Category Publisher Alex Allan
DTP Designer Lauren Egan
Production Rochelle Talary

First published in Great Britain in 2006 by
Dorling Kindersley Limited
80 Strand, London WC2R ORL

06 07 08 09 10 10 9 8 7 6 5 4 3 2 1

ISBN-13 978-1-40531-421-3

ISBN-10 1-4053-1421-4

Colour reproduction by Media Development and Printing Ltd., UK
Printed and bound in Italy by L.E.G.O.

ACKNOWLEDGEMENTS
The Publishers would like to thank Kamaria Hill, Kate Lewine, Gail Harrison,
Lori Forte, Cindy Slattery and Tom Cordone from Fox; Blue Sky Studios; and
Artful Doodlers Ltd. for the additional artworks.

Discover more at
www.dk.com